A TOWN NAMED WAR BOY

ROSS MUELLER

CURRENCY PRESS
SYDNEY

ATYP
Australian Theatre
for Young People

CURRENT THEATRE SERIES

First published in 2015
by Currency Press Pty Ltd,
PO Box 2287, Strawberry Hills, NSW, 2012, Australia
enquiries@currency.com.au
www.currency.com.au
in association with Australian Theatre for Young People, Sydney.

Reprinted 2018

Cataloguing-in-publication data for this title is available from the National
Library of Australia website: www.nla.gov.au

Typeset by Dean Nottle for Currency Press..
Cover photograph by John Tsiavis.
Front cover shows Joshua Brennan.

Currency Press acknowledges the Traditional Owners of the Country on which
we live and work. We pay our respects to all Aboriginal and Torres Strait
Islander Elders, past and present.

Contents

A Town Named War Boy was first produced by the Australian Theatre for Young People and the State Library of New South Wales at the State Library of New South Wales, Sydney, on 29 April 2015, with the following cast:

SNOW	Joshua Brennan
JOHN	Simon Croker
TOM	Brandon McClelland
HUDDO	Edward McKenna

Director, Fraser Corfield
Designer, Adrienn Lord
Lighting Designer, Emma Lockhart-Wilson
Composer, Steve Francis
Sound Designer, Alistair Wallace
Assistant Directors, Lisa Mumford, Julia Patey

CHARACTERS

SNOW

TOM

HUDDO

JOHN

SETTING

A huge desk that is also a boat. The desk is covered in diaries and papers that seem to fill the room. The diaries and papers also become the sea.

A NOTE ON THE TEXT

When a [/] occurs within the dialogue, it indicates the point of interruption or overlap for the following line of dialogue.

This play went to press before the end of rehearsals and may differ from the play as performed.

PROLOGUE

Lights up on SNOW. *He is barefoot on the sand. The sound of waves and distant gulls. He smiles. He draws with his toe in the wet sand and then he speaks and kneels and writes with the index finger of his left hand.*

SNOW: The contents of this book…
Have been written at random.
Yeah…
So please… do not take… offence, at any *personal* remarks.

> *Pause. He smiles.*

This town… alright.
Our town is…
Full of silence.

> *The sound of little waves.*

This place, which gave me my great chance in life—now…

> *Pause. He stops writing.*

I daydream now of…

> *He starts to build a little sandcastle with his left hand.*

Open plains and drifting.
Mates,
cobbers…
My boys.
I am… a little wild man!
Cold, cold and muddy.
Wallowing in the mud like… mad—bloody—pigs!

> *He regards the castle.*

Where are my war boys now?

SCENE ONE

SNOW *approaches the desk with caution. He takes a chocolate from his pocket and starts to eat. He scans some of the other documents.*

Some sketches. He picks up a small red book. Opens it carefully. He reads the first line quietly to himself. Closes the book in his hands, smiles and puts the diary into his breast pocket. TOM *rises from beneath the books and papers. Pause.*

TOM: What's the matter, are you scared?
SNOW: No.
TOM: Yes, you are.

    Beat.

SNOW: Is this your desk?
TOM: Yes.
SNOW: Why is it covered in bodies?
TOM: What?… This is paper.
SNOW: Diaries.
TOM: Purchased by the library. These are books not bodies.
SNOW: Looks like people.

    The sound of water lapping begins.

TOM: Is that what you think?
SNOW: I know.
TOM: What do you think you know? [*Pause.*] 'Nature is sad.' I can see it in your eyes.
SNOW: Those words do not belong to you.
TOM: Come inside—let's begin.
SNOW: Can you hear water?
TOM: No.
SNOW: Listen…
HUDDO: Signaller…
TOM: What?
SNOW: Over the top!

    A whistle.

SCENE TWO

*Men roar into the fire of battle—*SNOW *throws the desk over on itself, papers fly everywhere and the desk becomes a boat. All jump in the boat. Water lapping. They sit in silence. The night rocks them gently.*

Little waves are made up from the text of the diaries. We can just make out the men's faces.

HUDDO: Bloody freezing.

JOHN: Blood / oath.

SNOW: Typical.

HUDDO: What does that mean?

SNOW: This was all your idea.

JOHN: Me?

SNOW: Not you! Him!

JOHN: Yeah! That's right. [*To* HUDDO] He's right! This is your fault!

HUDDO: My?

JOHN: Freeze the balls off a brass monkey out here.

HUDDO: All I said, was we should get / involved together!

ALL: Get involved together.

HUDDO: Not my fault you're a mob of sheep.

SNOW: Bloody brilliant this is.

HUDDO: Nobody's twisting your arm, mate!

SNOW: How could I possibly say no?

JOHN: Listen—

HUDDO: What?

SNOW: There—what's he saying?

     Beat.

TOM: Who?

SNOW: Thought I could hear a voice.

HUDDO & JOHN: [*together, in a whisper*] Murder… bloody murder…

     Pause.

SNOW: You hear that?

TOM: Hear what?

SNOW: In the darkness. What are they saying?

TOM: You hearing voices now, Snow?

SNOW: Maybe.

HUDDO: He's as mad as a bag full of cats!

TOM: That's / enough, Huddo.

SNOW: You don't know what you're talkin' about—

HUDDO: He's hearing voices in the darkness!

SNOW: You need to understand something, buddy.

HUDDO: And what's that?

SNOW: You're the only bloody head case in this godforsaken boat!

HUDDO: Oh, is that right?! / Is that a fact, is it?

SNOW: Just start listening—that's all I'm sayin'!

HUDDO: I don't need you to tell me that I'm going round the bend!

SNOW: You've got a brain like a squashed tomato!

HUDDO: Are you havin' a bloody go at me?!

SNOW: Mate, I will deck you if you wanna try me.

TOM: / Cut it out!

HUDDO: Yeah, alright! Let's go! / Let's do it!

SNOW: Don't try and stop him, Tom.

TOM: You're not gonna fight in my boat, in the middle of this night!

SNOW: Why not?!

JOHN: Yeah, why not?!

SNOW: He's been buggin' me for months!

HUDDO: For bloody *months*, now is it?

SNOW: Shut ya mouth, ya drongo!

HUDDO: Snow! You did your best… Okay?

SNOW: My best?!… That's it? My best?

TOM: He's right.

SNOW: And that's enough. Is it?… We do our best. Our best… So… Now what? We go home? Run away? We give up and leave your mates out here?… It's freezing.

HUDDO: They brought us here to die, Snow. This is the beach. This is War Boy.

SNOW: I don't believe that for a second.

HUDDO: Don't be a fool.

SNOW: It's not a real place.

HUDDO: Yes / it is.

SNOW: No, it's not.

JOHN: Are you calling him a liar?

SNOW: I'm saying he doesn't know the truth!

HUDDO: I know there's a town called Hell.

SNOW: Alright then! How can we escape?

JOHN: Escape?

HUDDO: From here?

SNOW: Please? Help me!… I hate this life alone.
HUDDO: Signaller. I've made a decision.

> HUDDO *leaps from the boat.*

SNOW: Huddo!

> SNOW *dives overboard and follows him into the water.*

SCENE THREE

They come up gasping for oxygen.

HUDDO: Huddo Hutton!
SNOW: Address?
HUDDO: Any old place!
SNOW: The contents of this book have been / written at random.
HUDDO: Fourth of August, I throw in my lot with the army!
SNOW: For milk and tea and ice-cream!
HUDDO: Come on, boys! You gotta be in it!
SNOW: Here we go!
TOM: Just like that? You're off to a war?
HUDDO: We're gonna see the bloody world, Tom!
SNOW: I can't believe you / sometimes!
HUDDO: That's my boy!
SNOW: Count me in!
HUDDO: Here we go, lads! All together now!… We—eeeee!

> *They all join him in a rousing shouting chorus.*

ALL: [*sung*] We are the ragtime army!
　　　But we'll prove in a ragtime way!
　　　Tell Kaiser Bill and his naughty son
　　　That we'll win the blooming day!
　Hey!
HUDDO: Six a.m.!
SNOW: What?!
TOM: He needs his beauty sleep!
SNOW: Shut your trap, ya mongrel!
HUDDO: Fall in! / Come on, you lot! Shake a leg and look lively!
　We've got a war to get to on time, you know? Fall in, fall in!
　That's an order! Here we go!

SNOW: Signalling!—Another language—I wonder if I shall ever be any good at it. Three days training at the ranges. My first shot with the rifle—can't stand the damned noise.

HUDDO: Hit the target.

SNOW: Don't know how I managed that.

HUDDO: You done alright.

SNOW: I don't reckon I can shoot a man.

HUDDO: You'll do alright. I'll / watch out for you.

SNOW: Huddo?… Where are you, mate?!

HUDDO: I'm right here, Snowy! By the seaside! Quick march!

They start whistling a marching song underneath.

JOHN: Full equipment, pack and sea bags—impossible to stand up, it is so slippery. March off from Broadmeadow Station; fall down and get up caked with mud. All the way to Port Melbourne I write farewell notes on bits of paper. I give them out to strangers on the stations as we pass through.

SNOW: What's he doing that for?

HUDDO: What are you doing that for?

JOHN: So that they can post them for me—hope that they will reach.

HUDDO: He reckons they're gonna post them for him.

SNOW: You're jokin'.

HUDDO: That's what he said,

SNOW: He's mental.

HUDDO: How about 'ambitious'?

JOHN: May be a long time before I get another chance to write.

HUDDO: Port Melbourne!

SNOW: Embark on transport.

HUDDO: A White Star Liner—

SNOW: *Ceramic*.

HUDDO: This!—is a very fine ship.

JOHN: At one p.m. we steam away—

HUDDO: No civilians on the wharf.

JOHN: Only the Harbour Master and labourers to wave adieu.

HUDDO: He's throwing those notes down to them now too—you see him?

SNOW: Ambition?

HUDDO: No, mate, that's bloody disturbing.

SNOW: [*to* JOHN] How the hell did you get in the army, son?

JOHN: My mother signed a letter.

SNOW: [*to* HUDDO] Like it was a school excursion.

JOHN: I'll be seventeen in June.

SNOW: My God.

JOHN: I know how to shoot. My uncle taught me.

SNOW: You from the bush?

JOHN: Riverina.

HUDDO: We better stick together, I reckon.

SNOW: Christ.

JOHN: Sounds good to me.

SNOW: Right. Thanks, Huddo.

HUDDO: He's gonna need protection.

SNOW: Yeah—well, he's got a whole bloody army to do that now.

JOHN: Goodbye Australia!

SNOW: Goodbye Australia?

JOHN: Hello war!

SNOW: Here we go.

JOHN: Rest of the day arranging kit on board. Noise and confusion—

HUDDO: Fixing up / hammocks—

SNOW: Picking out the / best spots—

JOHN: Getting in each / other's way.

HUDDO: Such a confined space!

SNOW: Three thousand souls on board *Ceramic*. Nowhere quiet to think.

JOHN: I meet bloke named Bell.

HUDDO: He is very bitter against the Germans—

JOHN: And he always has a knife—

HUDDO: Which he is always sharpening.

JOHN: He says he will show the Germans no mercy.

HUDDO: No mercy?

JOHN: Looks like he means it.

HUDDO: Means what, mate?

JOHN: Murder. Bloody murder.

SNOW: Just outside town, dripping with blood—boys walk in the sand at midnight.

HUDDO: What's that?

SCENE FOUR

Doctor's room. SNOW *starts another chocolate.*

TOM: Shall we?
SNOW: What?
TOM: Make a start? On you.
SNOW: Why me?
TOM: You've got to get it moving.
SNOW: Am I constipated?
TOM: You know what's wrong with you.
SNOW: There's nothing wrong with me.

        Pause.

TOM: You can leave at any time you like.
SNOW: I just bloody might!
TOM: Go ahead.
SNOW: I will.
TOM: Well, good.
SNOW: Right.
TOM: Goodbye.
SNOW: Goodbye.
TOM: Shut the door on the way out, will you?
SNOW: Thanks for bloody nothin'!
TOM: It was my pleasure!
SNOW: Not at all! It was mine!
TOM: I insist!
SNOW: I don't care!
TOM: Yes you do!
SNOW: I don't need your shit in my life, I'm goin' to the beach!

        Pause.

TOM: You're not moving. [*Beat.*] You appear to be rooted to the spot.
    Like a—
SNOW: Eucalyptus?
TOM: I was going to say—a—ghost gum.

        Beat.

SNOW: Why didn't you shake my hand? [*Beat.*] You didn't even shake my hand. When we met just now. Why not? What's wrong? What's wrong with you, Tommy? We're not in the army now, mate! We're all on Civvie Street and *civilians* shake each other by the bloody hand, mate. That's how you greet someone in peacetime. That's what you do! When you meet an old cobber, you stick out a mitt! Shake a paw, son! Put it there, pal! Show respect! Show me that you're fair bloody dinkum! This lifeboat is going down!

TOM: / Take it easy, Snowy.

SNOW: How many bodies are you hiding under / here?!

TOM: Stop! You're at peace.

SNOW: Peace?!

TOM: Yes! This is peacetime.

SNOW: Is it?

> *Beat.*

TOM: I heard a bloke say the war will be over before we get there.

SNOW: What?

TOM: I said—

SCENE FIVE

On the deck—sunning themselves.

TOM: I heard a bloke say the war will be over before we get there.

SNOW: Over before we get there?

TOM: That's what he said.

> *Pause.*

SNOW: Well, that's a bloody awful thing to say.

HUDDO: Perish the bloody / thought!

JOHN: Who the hell would say a terrible thing like / that?!

HUDDO: Why would God do a bloody horrible thing like that?

TOM: It would be the merciful thing to do.

HUDDO: Don't you want the adventure, mate?

TOM: You think this is a bloody joke?

> *Beat.*

SNOW: No joke in serving your / King and Country.

HUDDO: Too right, too bloody right. What kind of patriot are you?

JOHN: What are you scared of, Tommy?

TOM: I never said I was scared.

HUDDO: You're worse than the bloody Poms!

TOM: How dare you! / Comparing me to the bloody—Poms?! You dirty bloody mongrel! Put your dukes up right now! Let's sort this out! Once and for all!

HUDDO: Oh yeah, oh yeah? If I could see, you reckon? Okay. You know what?! I reckon you're bloody terrified. You're not a man, you're a bloody mouse!

TOM: I'm as good a man as any one of you mob!

HUDDO: All I can see is a boy.

> *Pause.*

> HUDDO *lunges at* TOM *and kisses him and the boys break into laughter.*

TOM: Cheeky bastard, isn't / he?

HUDDO: I'm going to fight for our freedom, Tom.

JOHN: Is that why we're on a boat?

SNOW: Holy Mother of God.

HUDDO: It's a great adventure, Johnny.

JOHN: Yes, it is!

HUDDO: Lie back and soak up the sunshine.

JOHN: Alright, I will!

SNOW: Glad that's settled.

HUDDO: Give it a rest, Snow.

SNOW: Sorry, mate—cabin fever.

JOHN: This morning I nearly fainted.

HUDDO: You serious?

JOHN: Yes I—am.

HUDDO: What's wrong?

SNOW: He's light-headed.

JOHN: I can't sleep.

TOM: Tried counting girlfriends?

JOHN: I don't have any—

SNOW: You can borrow some of mine if you think it might help.

JOHN: Thanks, Snow, I just might I think. Five nights in a row now.

TOM: What's wrong?

JOHN: My imagination. It's a little—wild.

HUDDO: What the hell are you imagining?

JOHN: I just can't stop myself from thinking—

SNOW: What?

JOHN: That I many never paint again.

    Beat.

SNOW: Did he say 'paint'?

TOM: He said paint.

SNOW: He can't stop himself from painting?

TOM: Thinking about painting, so he's not sleeping and he's fainting.

SNOW: You're joking.

TOM: No, it's serious.

HUDDO: Painting?

JOHN: That's right.

SNOW: You taking the piss?

JOHN: No, I went just after breakfast.

SNOW: What?

HUDDO: You an artist?

JOHN: I was. I am. I don't know anymore. It's getting too much for me.

SNOW: You're a painter?

JOHN: I'm an artist.

SNOW: Well, what are you doing in the army?

JOHN: Serving my country—like you.

SNOW: Listen, Van Gogh, you're crazy!

JOHN: I'm not crazy!

SNOW: No need to cut off an ear about it!

JOHN: I'm not mad! I just have to paint!

TOM: And—I have to sing!

HUDDO: I have to drink!

SNOW: I have to satisfy women. Doesn't mean kids like you have to go fighting!

JOHN: I'm as strong as any man here.

SNOW: That's not the point.

JOHN: I can shoot. I can ride. I can run.

SNOW: And you're a signaller.

JOHN: You don't think I'm going to be much use.

SNOW: Come on, mate! No… you're useless!

JOHN: Very well. I shall take your advice and just give it up.

HUDDO: You can't give up now!

JOHN: Why not?

HUDDO: We're in the middle of the bloody ocean.

JOHN: So what?

HUDDO: We're not even halfway there!

JOHN: But I'm useless!

SNOW: That's what I'm trying to tell you.

JOHN: Good luck.

> JOHN *runs to jump overboard. The men clamour to catch him and subdue him. There is a lot of commotion. They settle him.*

HUDDO: Come on, Vincent. Have a chocolate.

SCENE SIX

Doctor's room. SNOW *starts another chocolate.*

TOM: I can offer you a choice between the chair or the couch.

SNOW: Is this a test?

TOM: No. It's an offer of the chair or the couch. I think you… This is not a test.

> SNOW *sits.*

SNOW: Did I pass?

TOM: You're making progress. Are you comfortable?

SNOW: Yes.

TOM: Alright. You can begin.

SNOW: How do I do that?

TOM: It doesn't matter. There are no wrong answers. There are no wrong recollections.

SNOW: I don't know what you want me to say.

TOM: Tell me what you think about being back home.

> *Pause.*

SNOW: I like the beach.
TOM: Very good.

Pause.

SNOW: That's it?
TOM: What do you do—when you go to the beach?
SNOW: Dunno.
TOM: Try and be specific if you can.
SNOW: I go there in the darkness.
TOM: By yourself?
SNOW: No.

HUDDO *and* JOHN *enter the scene. They sit with* SNOW.

TOM: Who goes with you?

Pause.

SNOW: I met another angel last night.
TOM: Another angel?

Beat.

SNOW: Yeah.
TOM: At the beach?

Pause.

SNOW: She had skin like silk and eyes like / sapphires and—ohhh…
    She was perfect.
JOHN: Another angel, Snow? That's amazing. You're my hero.
SNOW: I'm a lucky man, Johnny. / What can I tell you? I live a
    charmed life.
JOHN: Well—yes, that's one way of putting it—'lucky' for sure.
TOM: Who's Johnny? [*Pause.*] You said—'I'm a lucky man, Johnny'.
    Who's Johnny? … Am I Johnny?
SNOW: No.
TOM: You sure?

Beat.

SNOW: Yeah.
JOHN: Where did you meet this new angel, Snowy?
SNOW: Nah—you don't wanna know.
JOHN: Details.

TOM: Tell me about the angels.

HUDDO: Where'd you meet her?

SNOW: She saw us when we were marching.

JOHN: They love the boys in uniform. / Don't they?

HUDDO: How would you bloody know, Johnno?

JOHN: / I know.

HUDDO: They don't ever notice you, when you're marching!

JOHN: They notice me—

HUDDO: You're bloody dreamin', mate.

JOHN: I have a few pretty faces / turn my way!

HUDDO: Oh! Listen to bloody Romeo over here, will ya? Romeo of
  Rose Bloody Bay!

JOHN: Now, why would / you say somethin' like that?!

SNOW: Hey, fellas?… This is my story, isn't it?

TOM: Yes.

SNOW: What?

TOM: This is your story… You can tell me.

   Pause.

SNOW: I think I have fallen in love.

TOM: / Fallen in love?

HUDDO: Again? / He says it! He falls in love every Saturday night!

JOHN: Bloody hell, Snow!

TOM: That's marvellous.

SNOW: It's bloody serious!

HUDDO: The serial offender!

TOM: You're a lucky man to find love in this town!

JOHN: How many sweethearts have you got on the go now, mate?

HUDDO: Three or four, I'd say.

JOHN: This is number five!

HUDDO: He's been counting!

SNOW: My soul cannot keep count!

HUDDO: Do they all know you're such a firecracker, Snow?

SNOW: I cannot leave affection unfulfilled!

HUDDO: But what will they do without you? Who are they going to
  dream about when they lay down / their pretty little heads?

SNOW: I refuse to imagine. I love each with all my human heart.

HUDDO: I feel nothing but pity for these poor lovely things.

SNOW: And, I feel the same for you, mate. [*Pause.*] But I will return to hold their hands. This is a promise I make to each one and they give me a smile. They give me a kiss. [*Beat.*] She gives me a reason to live.

TOM: That's good.

SNOW: What's good?

TOM: Love. This is good. Love is healthy.

SNOW: So why did you refuse to shake my hand?

> *Beat.*

TOM: I didn't refuse—I didn't know what… I didn't realise you were an amputee.

SNOW: I'm your first?

TOM: Yes.

SNOW: I'll be gentle.

TOM: How did you lose your hand?

> *Pause.*

SNOW: My God… My God… I've done my duty. I've done my duty, haven't I, Tommy Boy?

> *Pause.*

> SNOW *stands and starts to move his arms as if he is signalling. This action continues throughout the following scene.*

SCENE SEVEN

On the ship.

JOHN: Instruction in signalling!

SNOW: Crikey.

HUDDO: If you by some minor miracle you learn the language of semaphore, and for some mystical reason beyond all comprehension a lowly cove such as yourself is put in charge of a signal station…!

SNOW: Yes, sir?

HUDDO: In the event of a message having to be sent which will entail great danger to the messenger, you may not take it! I repeat! You may—not—take it! Do you understand me?!

SNOW: Yes, sir!

HUDDO: Very good.

SNOW: Sir?

HUDDO: What is it, man?

SNOW: Sir, what should I do?

HUDDO: You must—send a man who is under you!

SNOW: I didn't realise there was anybody under me, sir.

HUDDO: This is the army, man.

SNOW: Yes, sir!

HUDDO: There's always somebody beneath you! Now! Breakfast! Clean up! Signal practice and then some well-earned nosh! Look lively!

SNOW: Yes, sir.

HUDDO: Christmas Day today and so we've got a little extra for you.

SNOW: Sir?

HUDDO: Fruit. Oranges and lemons. Mhmmm. A nutritious Christmas!

JOHN: A happy Christmas, one and all.

SNOW: A bloody orange?

HUDDO: Enjoy!

> *Pause.*

JOHN: December twenty-six.

HUDDO: Party's over! Fall in! Let's have you! Rise and shine!

> *Water lapping.*

> SNOW *breaks from the scene and walks to the sand.*

> *His castle has been trampled; he starts to build it again.*

SCENE EIGHT

Doctor's office.

SNOW: Empty of young men and laughter. [*He keeps building, then quietly*] Signaller…

> *He stands back to admire his work, he is unimpressed with his castle.*

God in heaven, this is awful.

TOM: Really? I quite like it myself.

SNOW: How many forests did they cut down to build these legs for
   you?

TOM: I don't think it's that unusual, is it?

SNOW: Takin' up half the room.

TOM: This seems to be a problem for you.

SNOW: No.

TOM: You're preoccupied.

SNOW: No, sir. It's just a desk, sir.

   Beat.

TOM: How would you like me to refer to you?

SNOW: Me mates call me Snow.

TOM: Snow? Or Snowy?

SNOW: Either one. I'm not the fussy type.

TOM: Can I call you Snow?

SNOW: No.

TOM: Why not?

SNOW: You're not me mate.

TOM: Not yet.

SNOW: You're not my mate.

TOM: So, what would you like me to call you?

SNOW: Simon.

HUDDO: Simon?

SNOW: Bloody Simon, alright!

TOM: Alright, / Simon.

HUDDO: Simple bloody Simon—

SNOW: That's what my mother named me.

TOM: It's a good name. /

HUDDO: Biblical.

SNOW: Simon was an apostle.

HUDDO: Are you?

SNOW: Don't be a moron.

HUDDO: Do you know Jesus?

SNOW: I've got a good mind to smack you right in the moosh.

TOM: Simon?

SNOW: What?

TOM: Are you—?

SNOW: A disciple?

TOM: No—

SNOW: Fisherman by trade, as I understand.

TOM: Yes, I think / that's right.

SNOW: That's an honest living, isn't it?

JOHN: He had a boat.

HUDDO: And he smelt of fish apparently.

SNOW: [*to* HUDDO] I'm going to ignore you and you're going to disappear.

TOM: No. I'm not. [*Pause.*] Do you know why you've been referred to me, Simon?

SNOW: I got the letter.

TOM: It's a referral.

SNOW: What are you trying to inseminate?

TOM: I'm not trying to insinuate, / anything.

SNOW: I think you are.

HUDDO: / You really are a class-A idiot sometimes.

SNOW: You're inseminating / something and I don't like it.

TOM: Simon—I don't understand / what you're talking about.

SNOW: Who has a desk this bloody big in their bloody office?! Fair dinkum!

TOM: / You really don't like my desk, do you?

SNOW: I mean, what kind of a man has something this big in bloody public? It's embarrassing.

TOM: / We're not in public.

SNOW: [*to* HUDDO] / What is he trying to compensate for, Huddo?!

HUDDO: He's trying to bloody help you! You're out of your bloody tree, mate.

TOM: I'm sorry? / Who's Huddo?… Simon, are you hearing voices?

SNOW: You're 'in charge', is that it? You're my commanding officer and this is the way it's happening, right?!

TOM: Is that what you're reading into / my desk?

SNOW: Listen!… I'm just giving you the facts! Okay? I am letting you know that I'm no dill. You big bastard. Pick me / off as soon as I lift my head. We are vampires, in our nests all day! We do our dirty work at night!

TOM: You don't have to upset yourself, Simon. How do you think you ended up here?

SNOW: I volunteered!

TOM: For this?

SNOW: I am a patriot! I love life! I was born with the sun on my face! Aussie boys! Anchors aweigh!

HUDDO: All is well aboard the *Star of England*! /

SNOW: Fighting tonight for the Lightweight Championship!

> SNOW *leaps to his feet and starts sparring with* HUDDO.

SCENE NINE

On the ship.

JOHN: [*loudly coaching* SNOW] You gotta create an illusion of strength! He's a big brick bastard this dirty Russian shithouse, he's not gonna go down easy! You gotta lay him out flat! Bang!

HUDDO: He looks bigger than a Lightweight.

JOHN: Don't worry about / that, sunshine.

HUDDO: Bigger they are / the harder you hit 'em.

JOHN: Rush him from the bell.

HUDDO: Crowd him the corner.

JOHN: Defend, defend and then attack!

HUDDO: Or attack, attack, defend! Either way. Okay?!

JOHN: Got that?!

SNOW: Got what? /

TOM: Ding, ding!

HUDDO: There's the bell!

SNOW: Hell!

HUDDO: Oh, / that must've bloody hurt.

JOHN: Didn't stand a bloody chance.

HUDDO: You right, Snow? Can you stand up?

> SNOW *is laid out flat on his back. He is breathing very heavily and then:*

SNOW: Did I win?

HUDDO: You're getting better.

JOHN: Put up a good show.

HUDDO: Bloody murder…

SNOW: What's that?

HUDDO: I said we'll spend some solid time together, working on your defence.

SNOW: Good. Good, thanks... A fortnight today I was at Manly with Elsie and Muriel. Weather—beautiful—sea—like glass.

HUDDO: Concussed again.

JOHN: Yep.

HUDDO: I'll get the salts.

> HUDDO *leaves and* JOHN *is alone with* SNOW—*seagulls.*

JOHN: How do they get so far out to sea like this?

SNOW: The birds?

JOHN: Long way from home.

SNOW: Suppose they follow the fish.

JOHN: Do they eat fish for their dinner, do they?

SNOW: I don't know. Somebody has to.

JOHN: I reckon if I was a seagull... I don't think I would come out this far.

SNOW: Stick to the coast?

JOHN: Love the beach.

SNOW: Too scared to leave it?

JOHN: There's nothing wrong with being scared.

SNOW: What are you accusing me of?

TOM: Nothin'.

SNOW: I'm a fighter.

TOM: Yes, I can see that.

SNOW: I'm gonna fight the whole way over and the whole time there and the whole way home again.

TOM: Yeah.

SNOW: I will.

TOM: I bet you will too, Snow.

> *Beat.* TOM *leaves* SNOW *alone.* SNOW *sits up and finds some tobacco. He begins to roll himself a smoke with one hand.*

HUDDO: [*in the distance*] Signaller!...

> SNOW *hears the voice.*

[*In the distance*] Signaller!...

> SNOW *is terrified.*

SCENE TEN

TOM: What's wrong, Simon? [*Pause.*] You're shaking.

SNOW: What?

TOM: You can smoke outside, when we're finished.

SNOW: Smoke?

TOM: Not in here.

SNOW: Oh.

JOHN: I didn't smoke before I joined up.

TOM: A lot of chaps take up the habit.

JOHN: Tobacco settles the nerves.

TOM: Simon?

SNOW: Snow.

TOM: Snow, can you please not smoke right now?

HUDDO: The following cigarettes are being issued to me during my services in the army: Hagdens. Tabs. Rough Riders. Ruby Queen! / Three Witches, Trumpeters, Flags, Arf O Moss, All Arms, Wild Woodbines, Honeydews, Roll Calls, Classico Critics, B.D.V.'s, Glory Boys, Britannias, Black Cats, British Standard, Derbys, Scissors, Red Hussiers, Ring Ludd Campaigners, Pinnace, Drapkins and bloody Volunteers!

SNOW: Hagdens. Tabs. Rough Riders. / Ruby Queen, Three Witches, Trumpeters, Flags, Arf O Moss, All Arms, Wild Woodbines, Honeydews, Roll Calls, Classico Critics, B.D.V.'s, Glory Boys, Britannias, British Standard, Derbys, Scissors, Red Hussiers, Ring Ludd Campaigners, Pinnace, Drapkins and fucking Volunteers!

JOHN: Glory Boys, Britannias, Black Cats, Wild Woodbines, Hagdens. Rough Riders. Ruby Queen, Three Witches, Trumpeters, Flags, Arf O Moss, All Arms, Honeydews, Roll Calls, B.D.V.'s, British Standard, Derbys, Campaigners, Pinnace, Drapkins and these bloody Volunteers!

> *Pause.*

TOM: I might join you in a durry. How about that?

> *Beat.* SNOW *hands the tobacco to* TOM. *All four roll their smokes together.*

You know... I saw action.

SNOW: Yeah.

TOM: I was at Lone Pine.

SNOW: You too?

TOM: Yes.

SNOW: Didn't see you there.

TOM: No.

SNOW: Lone Pine.

TOM: Feels like yesterday.

SNOW: No. Forever.

TOM: I used to think to myself—when we were taking fire: 'The world doesn't know if we're alive or if we're dead'.

HUDDO: Will we ever smell Australia again?

JOHN: Feeling very lonely with a greasy smile.

HUDDO: Sighing and almost crying—

JOHN: Cursing and then smiling—

TOM: I took this job with both eyes open.

SNOW: Now, I cannot even close them for sleep.

HUDDO: Stuck here in this town—

JOHN: No escape, no shelter.

HUDDO: Forever on guard and watching—

JOHN: My enemy…

HUDDO: This is hell.

TOM: Let's step outside.

> *Music begins. They walk out on deck and the four of them lean against the rail together. They sing.*

SONG: 'Australia Will Be There'

> When old John Bull is threatened
> By foes on land or sea
> His colonial sons are ready
> And at his side will be
> From Africa, India and Canada
> Come men, to do or die
> And motherland is glad to hear
> Australia's battle—cry!
>
> Rally round the banner of your country
> Take the field with brothers o'er the foam

On land or sea
Where'er you be
Keep your eye on Germany
But England, home and beauty
Have no cause to fear
Should auld acquaintance be forgot
No, no, no! Australia will be there.

JOHN: Land! Land ho! We made it!

They cheer and chatter.

SCENE ELEVEN

HUDDO: Our ship swings into the harbour and / anchors.

JOHN: It isn't long till rumours are flying—

SNOW: We are going to disembark and …

JOHN: Go into action.

SNOW: Tommy Boy!

HUDDO: There's no turning back from here now. Three cheers for the King! Hip hip!

They cheer three cheers and climb to the top of the boat to get a better view of the action in the water below them.

SNOW: Locals swarming around the boat trying to sell / inferior goods.

HUDDO: Like Johnny Walker, I'm still going strong! We hit Cairo like a train!

Blinding lights up on the men—they wear fezzes, sunglasses and cigars.

SNOW: Woah! Cairo!

HUDDO: / Cairo!

SNOW: Cairo! You city of sin and shame!

HUDDO: I love every disgusting inch of you! Every dirty little alley, every dusty backroom bar—the pyramids are marvellous, but I could spend the rest of my days quite happily in the arms of your temptation! This is the home of the most—the most degrading sights of the universe! I love you all!

JOHN: I never wish to witness again.

HUDDO: What's wrong? Have you finally gone mad, Vincent?

JOHN: I've got a toothache!

SNOW: He's got a toothache.

HUDDO: I can show you a fine way to make your pain disappear, my
     friend!

JOHN: No, no—

SNOW: Life here is not too bad! But the dust and the sandstorms are a
     bugger.

JOHN: I don't like this place—

SNOW: Look at the bright side!

JOHN: There is no bright side to this / country, Snow!

SNOW: Oh, come on, mate, I have come to the conclusion that Egypt
     is the best washerwoman country in the globe. Dry in two hours
     and the sun draws the dirt out.

HUDDO: That's the least of all her blessings!

SNOW: A sunny Sunday in Sunland!

JOHN: [*giving him two fingers*] This is how I feel about things arse-up
     here!

HUDDO: Let's go and get a skinful.

SNOW: Beer, beer glorious beer!

HUDDO: A bottle a day keeps the doctor away!

SNOW: Beer on the desert is bloody glorious off the ice!

HUDDO: Duck into Cairo—

JOHN: Too dangerous!

HUDDO: Take it easy!

JOHN: Last time we went in there was a riot between / the natives and
     their troops.

HUDDO: It was a row, it wasn't a riot!

JOHN: Two killed on Good Friday, Huddo!

HUDDO: So what?

SNOW: That's their business!

HUDDO: They're not Christian!

JOHN: I am!

SNOW: So what?

JOHN: My tooth is killing me—

SNOW: Because you're a Believer?

JOHN: His sacred day was well celebrated!

HUDDO: I never felt better!

SNOW: Nor thirstier!

HUDDO: Talk about dry!

JOHN: Camp is been hell, / great gusts of wind—sand, sand, sand everywhere.

HUDDO: Life is sweet when sweetness is on the menu. Out here it's what you make it!

JOHN: I make it sour—stuffy and sad.

HUDDO: Come on, Johnny—it's time to become a man!

JOHN: I'm only seventeen years old, thank you very much!

HUDDO: We should send you home to your mother!

JOHN: She knows where I am.

HUDDO: But she doesn't have to know what you're doing tonight!

SNOW: Let's go!

HUDDO: I am ready to report for duty!

SNOW: Atten-tion!

HUDDO: Shoulder arms!

JOHN: What are you two on about?

SNOW: It'd be a pity for you to end up in the trenches—alone. If you know what I'm saying?

JOHN: I won't be alone—I'll be with you blokes.

HUDDO: I think Snow is talking about—

SNOW: Your virginity.

JOHN: What about it?

SNOW: You still got it?

JOHN: So what?

SNOW: It's time to lose it.

JOHN: No way.

HUDDO: Come on, Johnny boy.

SNOW: You don't wanna die not knowing.

JOHN: Who says I'm going to die?!

SNOW: Just in case!

JOHN: I'm not showing up at the Pearly Gates, knowing that I've broken a Commandment!

HUDDO: God doesn't mind if you're a soldier.

JOHN: Is that true?

HUDDO: Ask him—he's a disciple.

JOHN: You?

SNOW: Yeah—no—as I understand it—there is a clause that can be activated in this type of circumstance and that is the clause that states that if a young man is in the company of a woman—before he—you know—has to hit the trenches—then you get a pass.
It's not a big thing—the Big Man is pretty understanding when it comes to this sort of caper.

JOHN: What if I catch a disease?

HUDDO: Penicillin was invented for moments exactly like this.

SNOW: Come on, Da Vinci. Let's go and dip your wick!

JOHN: No! I told you! My tooth is killing me. I don't want to spoil the—occasion.

HUDDO: Fair enough.

SNOW: That's your choice.

HUDDO: Personally—I choose the brothel over the molar—any day—but… Teeth are very handy in the trenches—so I can see why you wanna get them fixed.

SNOW: Yeah. Good luck, Fang.

HUDDO: We'll see you in the morning, Matisse!

SNOW: Don't wait up!

JOHN: You really are disgusting.

> JOHN *is alone. He draws in the sand with this boot.*

Nellie Breen…
Just a lass from the Riverina and in Cairo…
My heart is with her.
I wonder where she is.
Who she's with—and what they are doing.
I have a letter from Elsie, poor little girl…
'Boys will be boys', I tell her…
'—and we need to go fighting.'

> *Pause.*

But ohh… my tooth does ache.

SCENE TWELVE

JOHN *in the dentist chair.* TOM *is the dentist, Dr Garavedian.*

TOM: Lean back in the chair.

JOHN: Like this?

TOM: That's it. Open wide.

> JOHN *complies and* TOM *sets to work.*

TOM: Well—this is interesting.

JOHN: A strange and wonderful thing has happened—I go to have my teeth seen to and the dentist says—

TOM: It doesn't matter when you pay me.

JOHN: Really?

TOM: There is no rush.

JOHN: I might be leaving for the front tomorrow.

TOM: Tongue please—

JOHN: I said I might be leaving for the front at any time.

TOM: Never mind.

JOHN: Never mind?

TOM: Send me the money from Berlin!

JOHN: This is Dr Garavedian.

TOM: Good afternoon—wider please.

JOHN: He is a most charming and most hospitable man.

TOM: How do you like Cairo, Johnny?

JOHN: Sun, sand, sin and soldiers.

TOM: This is Egypt right now. But not always. What do you do in your army?

JOHN: Signaller.

TOM: And what do you do at home?

JOHN: I paint.

TOM: Ah. I thought so.

JOHN: Really?

TOM: I had a feeling—

JOHN: Why?

TOM: Your hands. They look—soft and—young.

> *Music begins.*

JOHN: I can shoot a gun.

TOM: I would hope so.

JOHN: I'm just saying—

TOM: Yes.

JOHN: You know?

TOM: I understand you are here to fight.

JOHN: On the battlefield, every burst of flame, every spurt of water, means death and worse. Other men talk about the impossible task up there. They reckon it's going to be—annihilation.

TOM: I understand.

JOHN: I don't believe it's that bad. [*Pause.*] Do you?

TOM: You know how to shoot a gun.

JOHN: What does annihilation mean?

TOM: It means it's good that you know how to shoot.

JOHN: I'm not scared.

TOM: Tongue.

JOHN: Like this?

TOM: Now this is going to hurt.

JOHN: Do you worst. Bloody hell!

TOM: Relax.

JOHN: Cripes!

TOM: You have a lot of decay—

JOHN: I know—

TOM: I'm going to have to do some extractions. Over the next few days.

JOHN: You're taking my teeth out?

TOM: Only the bad ones. You believe in the tooth fairy, Johnny?

JOHN: The what?

TOM: Tongue please.

JOHN: Argh.

TOM: That's better. You should brush.

JOHN: I do.

TOM: No you don't. I can see. I had some other Australians through here a little while ago—you might know them—they told me they once stayed in a town named—War Boy. Do you know it?

JOHN: Never heard of it.

TOM: Funny name for a town, don't you think?

JOHN: I'm not laughing.

TOM: How are you filling in your time here?

JOHN: We march.

TOM: In the desert?

JOHN: That's right.

TOM: In the heat of the day?

JOHN: We're getting fit. Flag drill studies.

TOM: Of course.

JOHN: And I sketch.

TOM: I'd love to see some of your work.

> HUDDO *and* SNOW *return to camp, drinking throughout the following.*

TOM: Tomorrow. Come over for lunch.

JOHN: Where?

TOM: To my house.

JOHN: What?

TOM: Tongue.

JOHN: Wait a second.

TOM: What is it?

JOHN: You want me to come to your house?

TOM: Yes. You're our guest. Come and meet my wife.

JOHN: You're married?

TOM: Yes, of course. We have an apartment in the Rue Magdeburg.

JOHN: And so I do. Day after day. I visit the Arab Museum. The Tombs of the Mamelukes. There is some wonderful work to be seen. Explore cafes alone and regular lunches with the wonderful Garavedians. Egypt is heaven. Like a family. They look after me. They fix my mouth and fill my belly. Showed me a different side of the world. He is a gentle husband and a father. I want to see the interior of some of the mosques… but then—

SNOW: Hot as love nine days / old.

HUDDO: Still drunk on desert gin and wine—

> *A whistle.*

JOHN: Standing orders issued.

> *They stop drinking.*

HUDDO: Soon we shall be upon the battlefield.

JOHN: I pray to God that I shall not be wanting when we are under fire.

> *A call to prayer is heard. This mixing with drums and whistles.*

SNOW: Brave men of Australia.

TOM: We are leaving for the trenches.
HUDDO: Signallers!
JOHN: Distance suggests to me—happy thoughts.
HUDDO: Signallers!
TOM: I pray to the Lord of War that the year 1917 may / bring peace!
HUDDO: Signallers?! Where are you mob?!
TOM: Here we go!
JOHN: This is it.
SNOW: This is war.

SCENE THIRTEEN

In the boat with torchlights.

HUDDO: Don't move.
JOHN: Don't smoke.
TOM: Don't speak.

        Pause.

SNOW: Closer—
TOM: Quiet.
SNOW: Voices in the darkness—
HUDDO: What was that?
SNOW: The wind.
HUDDO: What wind?
SNOW: Mine I reckon.
HUDDO: Don't be a dickhead.
SNOW: Mate, I'm / trying to provide a little levity in this—situation.
HUDDO: Why do you feel the need to try and turn everything into
    joke?
SNOW: Because I can't take much more of this bloody tension! /
JOHN: Shhhh.

        Pause.

HUDDO: What is it?…
SNOW: This is our grave, I reckon.

        They listen and begin to read the waves around them.

TOM: They're up there.
JOHN: Hear them?

HUDDO: I feel like I can touch 'em.
SNOW: Yeah.
HUDDO: So bloody close—mate.
SNOW: Breath of night is still.
JOHN: Trees.
HUDDO: What?
JOHN: Up ahead.
HUDDO: There aren't any trees up there, mate.
JOHN: Huddo—I can see the bloody huge bloody trees!
TOM: Mate, that's not trees—that's the beach and the cliffs ahead.
JOHN: Christ. Snow—
SNOW: Johnny?
JOHN: Snowy—
SNOW: Where are you, mate?
JOHN: I think I can see—
HUDDO: Murder—bloody—murder…
SNOW: I'm not going home without you.

The boat rocks and groans in the water.

TOM: Assembly is sounded—
SNOW: I have never seen it answered with such alacrity—
TOM: There is a loud cheer as we gather, pelting us like anything.
SNOW: The ships are keeping the tip of the ridges under a continual line of fire—
JOHN: We are told that we have landed / twenty thousand men.
SNOW: We are transferring into the boats. It is raining hot lead.

Silence. Then, as one, the boys yell as warriors and leap from their boat. They are terrified and murderous.

SCENE FOURTEEN

On the beachhead.

HUDDO: It's a relief to get ashore!
JOHN: Packed so tightly in the boats!
SNOW: The Turks pelted us hot and fast. / Hey, lads? They call that annihilation?!
JOHN: In jumping ashore I fall over, my kit is / so heavy; I couldn't get up without help—thank you, Huddo—Huddo!

HUDDO: You silly bugger—you could have copped it right there and then!

JOHN: I think you saved my life.

SNOW: Again?

TOM: It is a magnificent spectacle to see thousands of men rushing through the hail of death as though it is some big game—

HUDDO: These blokes don't know what fear means—

JOHN: In Cairo I was ashamed of you. Now I am proud to be one of them!

HUDDO: Thanks very much.

JOHN: Wish there wasn't quite such a damned noise with these guns.

SNOW: Get used to it, Johnny.

JOHN: It is sending me all to pieces—

HUDDO: / You'll be right.

JOHN: Don't think I shall ever make a soldier.

SNOW: We'll look after you.

JOHN: The beach is littered with wounded, some of them frightful spectacles.

HUDDO: What's a man gotta do to get a feed around here?

SNOW: / What's wrong with your bully beef?

JOHN: Indians bringing ammunition mules along the beach, / this scene of carnage worries them not at all.

HUDDO: I feel like a celebration!

SNOW: We've got a bit to get through yet!

HUDDO: But, Snowy! I am alive! All that bloody hail of lead?!… Missed me by that much! Ha! It is a soldier's life for me for sure! I pledge my future to the army today!

SNOW: Somebody smack him in the mouth, would you please?

TOM: Up the hill!

JOHN: I am given a pick to carry—halfway up I have to drop it.

HUDDO: You're gonna need this to get your trench in, Johnny.

JOHN: I know—

HUDDO: Give it here—I got the strength of / ten men tonight!

TOM: The lads on the top are glad to see us for they have been having an anxious time holding their position on the ridge—'Pope's Hill'—they had scarcely time to throw up more than a little earth to take cover behind.

SNOW: The noise is hell.

TOM: Boys disappear in the darkness and the smoke and then—

Pause.

SNOW: Silence.

Silence.

Cannot find any of the signallers of my station. I will look for my captain—they are sure to be with him. There is no time to wait for orders. I must work on my own initiative. In any case the captain will want a signaller with him. Some of the chaps are getting it—groans and screams everywhere… Calls for ammunition and stretcher-bearers. Though how they're going to carry stretchers along such precipitous and sandy slopes beats me. Now commencing to take some of the dead out of the trenches; this is horrible; I wonder how long I can stand it.

HUDDO: Signaller!

SNOW: It has been raining a little.

HUDDO: Signaller!

SNOW: Impossible to find my foothold!

HUDDO: Signaller!

SNOW: It's overwhelming!

HUDDO: Sunday! On the scene of death. It's murder! Bloody murder! No bodies move. No time. No peace.

SNOW: We see—

JOHN: The graves of many Turks, some with arms and legs protruding.

HUDDO: They had taken up positions behind little sand mounds—

SNOW: We see—

JOHN: Hundreds of boots tied in pairs—

SNOW: We see the grave of an officer.

HUDDO: Marked with a cross.

SNOW: He deserves his fate. He showed a white flag—and when our men ceased firing his rear lines still continued. His white flag appears to have been a regular part of his kit—he had a little khaki case for it.

JOHN: Thought this was going to be a grand adventure.

SNOW: Until we see it for ourselves. I fall in my tracks.

TOM: And how does that make you feel?

HUDDO: Signaller?
TOM: How does that make you feel?!

SCENE FIFTEEN

TOM *(as Dr Garavedian) and* SNOW *on the beach together.* SNOW *drops to the sand. Footprints in the sand. He traces a boot mark. He picks up a diary. He puts it in his pocket. He begins to build a sandcastle kingdom with his left hand. Garavedian continues while* SNOW *keeps building.* JOHN *and* HUDDO *come and help* SNOW *build the castles.*

TOM: Bursts of fire from our men, officers doing all they can to stop it—as we are getting short of ammunition. Bugling by Turks, makes me think of a Cairene bazaar; the idea of the bugles is supposed to impress us.
JOHN: I have been running despatches all night and in between endeavouring to make a dugout—I couldn't lift the pick so had to use my trenching tool.
HUDDO: Wonder what I am going to do for rations, / I had to throw mine out, it was too heavy for me to carry. Feeling very weak and tired.
TOM: April twenty-six. Pope's Hill. Daybreak. Down in the Valley, in the midst of this frightful hell of screaming shrapnel and heavy ordinance, the birds are chirping in the clear morning air and buzzing about from leaf to leaf.
SNOW: Signallers have been nearly all wiped out. I suppose I'll get my lead pill next.
HUDDO: Sunday. Raining like hell. Still playing soldiers and playing the game.
SNOW: All day long the big guns keep speaking and very loud / at that!
TOM: Soldier boy, soldier boy, what are you thinking of?!
SNOW: The boys went over last night and pushed Fritz back. We lost good men.

> *They cease building and look at the kingdom—pieces of paper fall to the earth like gentle snow on the beach.*

TOM: The enemy is dropping messages.

SNOW: Yes.

JOHN: From their planes?

SNOW: No from their bloody trenches, what do you reckon?

TOM: Alright—this goes on.

JOHN: What do the messages say?

SNOW: They're pamphlets—

HUDDO: They've printed some rubbish on them—

SNOW: It's propaganda!

JOHN: Tell me what the pamphlets say.

SNOW: What's the matter, can't you read?!

> *Pause—clearly he cannot.*

'WE WANT PEACE—AT ANY PRICE!'

JOHN: Peace?

SNOW: At any price…

JOHN: What does that…?

SNOW: Mean…?

JOHN: Yes! What is the price of peace?

HUDDO: Defeat!

SNOW: They will pay the price of defeat for peace?

JOHN: I suppose that's right.

SNOW: / You suppose… No, it does not. That's right, Huddo…
Bullshit!

HUDDO: Well—it doesn't make sense in the trenches. Not down the
back alleys and the little winding roads of war, this is pure—
bullshit. The best bloody liars in the world and they're bombing us
with pieces of paper?! For peace?!

SNOW: Don't they know we are at war?!

HUDDO: What's wrong with this bloody enemy?!

JOHN: But they could be dropping bombs, Huddo. What's the harm in
bits of paper?

SNOW: You reckon they wanna surrender?

JOHN: Why not?

SNOW: They're not gonna just give up!

TOM: Why not?

SNOW: Look what they've lost already! Blokes are dug in for the
long haul they're here for fightin' not for fun. This ain't no bloody
picnic. This is—fair dinkum. We're taking the trenches tonight.

Who's for a drink? Where's the rum? Come on, boys!… We have to enjoy it. For tomorrow night, we're gonna be inhabiting the ramparts. With the rats and the mud and the ghosts.

They open the rum and begin to drink.

TOM: In my mind, I am in a cafe in France. Irish, English, Scotch and Welsh. Australians and Canadians. All of us together and we're drunk as old Dave on a farmers' picnic.

They laugh.

SNOW: … Mary's a nice girl.

TOM: Here we go.

SNOW: Denise a sweet little thing of seventeen summers—

HUDDO: Denise, was that her name, was it?

SNOW: Not the one from that afternoon.

HUDDO: The one you were picking potatoes with?

SNOW: Marcella—

HUDDO: A labour of love.

SNOW: Believe me!

They laugh and then silence.

Remember on the boat coming over—commanding officer said to me after that fight with the big bloody Russian, 'Snowy… you're / as game as any man in France'…

JOHN & TOM: [*together*] / 'You're as game as any man in France'…

TOM: '… you're as game as any man in France'.

SNOW: Cheeky bastards.

HUDDO: It's a hard life, this soldiering job.

SNOW: The nights are like scorned love.

JOHN: Very cold—

SNOW: But it won't kill us for our hearts are big.

Silence and then quiet singing.

TOM: [*sung*] There's the captain as is our commander
　　　　　There's the bosun and all the ship's crew
　　　　　There's the first- and the second-class passengers
　　　　　Knows what we poor convicts go through.

ALL: [*sung*] Singing tooral liooral liaddity
　　　　　Singing tooral liooral liay

Singing tooral liooral liaddity
We're bound for—

Pause.

SNOW: And of course… it begins to rain.

It begins to rain.

SCENE SIXTEEN

SNOW *is working on the castles. In a trench.* HUDDO *leaps in out of nowhere.*

HUDDO: Alright, fellas, this is it, you gotta get some sleep.
SNOW: I'm okay—
HUDDO: No—
TOM: We can't sleep here.
HUDDO: This is good—
JOHN: This trench is too bloody shallow.
HUDDO: You're going to deepen it, my friend.
JOHN: Now? In the dark?
HUDDO: Don't talk. Just dig!
JOHN: What do you mean don't talk?
HUDDO: The Turks are just over here. If they hear you—they're going to kill you.
SNOW: If they can hear us talking… I reckon they might hear us digging too.
HUDDO: So stick the pick in quietly… if you wanna save you skins.

They try to dig quietly with their picks. SNOW *digs deeper and strikes something. He stops.*

TOM: Struck gold?
SNOW: Struck Turk.

They work to uncover the body of dead Turkish soldier—while TOM *continues:*

TOM: It's amazing how small the beach is. Don't you think? Simon?…
The whole pocket of land is—well—from the boat I thought I could fold it up and pop it into my kitbag.

There's a loss of control—that you feel when you're about to live in a place like that—where there are no laws beyond your own thoughts and feelings.

It's not a prison. It's a zoo—but there are no fences between the lions and the chimpanzees. There is just an understanding that we're sharing this soil—we're burying each other in wounded and we cannot do anything but fight to survive. Annihilation.

Physiological annihilation.

And this is how it begins.

HUDDO: While we were trying to root him out a Turkish bomb comes tumbling into the trench.

TOM: *Imshi! Imshi!*

JOHN: And we do *'imshi'* as quick as possible.

TOM: The Turks shell us with very large shells—

HUDDO: A Turkish aeroplane flies overhead and starts dropping bombs on our position! Gunboats shell back heavily!

TOM: Open up with very heavy fire.

SNOW: A Turk gives himself up as a prisoner.

HUDDO: He runs from his trench to ours under his own comrades' fire. He tumbles into our trench, is calling out:

JOHN: 'Allah, me finish fight!'

HUDDO: He kisses me. He cannot believe he is alive.

TOM: Shot at by his own men?

SNOW: He was deserting.

TOM: Running across No Man's Land.

SNOW: That's right.

TOM: That takes courage.

SNOW: The man's a coward.

TOM: What makes you think that?

SNOW: He is my enemy.

TOM: No sympathy?

SNOW: I don't feel a thing anymore.

TOM: You ever want to run?

SNOW: Are you mad?

Pause.

TOM: What stopped you?

SNOW: A man can stop himself… On the twenty-sixth we receive orders not to fire a shot. We are to remain absolutely silent. Artillery is silenced also. The cold is unbearable. At three a.m. the Turks send out a large patrol to find out what we are doing. They bundle up out of their trench, which is only about thirty yards from ours. Our orders are to let as many as possible get up before firing on them… and then… we fire!

HUDDO: Unleash hell!

SNOW: They find out to their sorrow—

HUDDO: We are here to fight to the death!

JOHN: Some get back to their trenches safe—

TOM: Some get back wounded and some—

SNOW: Lie here ever more. [*Pause.*] A man can stop himself.

He picks up the papers from the desk and drops them delicately like snow onto the ground.

White pages… blue pencil—little words and tiny records. Stolen moments of sanity and before the long dream of death.

SCENE SEVENTEEN

The sun begins to rise.

SNOW *stands and begins to signal as the scene continues.*

HUDDO: Daylight—bitter cold.

JOHN: Dead bodies in front of our trench are only partly covered.

HUDDO: The doctor wants to examine the corpses of those two Turks up there.

JOHN: Here?

HUDDO: Them two, that's right.

JOHN: What for?

HUDDO: Who's asking?

JOHN: I'm just saying—

HUDDO: Just what?

JOHN: What's he gonna find out that we don't already know?

HUDDO: Pull 'em in with grappling irons.

JOHN: Not—very respectful, Huddo.

HUDDO: Respect?

JOHN: For the dead?

HUDDO: You wanna leave them out there to rot?

> *Pause.*

TOM: After the examination they are buried side-by-side with our fellows.

HUDDO: A pitiful sight. Another hopeless dawn. No oranges here, just bully beef and biscuits.

JOHN: Miserable place.

HUDDO: But it could be worse.

SNOW: It could be worse?

HUDDO: That's right.

SNOW: Why did you say that?

HUDDO: To make you feel—reassured.

JOHN: It could be worse?

SNOW: How could it be any bloody worse?!

HUDDO: We could be those two bloody Turks!

SNOW: What? Dead? We could be dead?!

HUDDO: That's right!

SNOW: How is death worse than this?!

> *The men stand and look into the night sky. Their hands move quietly creating signals—almost involuntary movements now.*

JOHN: Beautiful.

HUDDO: Not a patch on the Southern Cross.

JOHN: Quiet.

SNOW: I can hear you both. I know you're out there.

> *Pause.*

JOHN: Nothin' out here but the rain.

> *Pause.*

TOM: The stench from Lone Pine is—abominable. Inhuman. Wipe the scenes away.

> *Pamphlets begin to fall to earth.*

HUDDO: You have gotta be bloody joking.

SNOW: How much is '… any price…'?

HUDDO: Sundown.

SNOW: I go to headquarters. See if there are any further messages. On my way I'm told to take cover, snipers have got much worse. One man pulled me into his dugout—

TOM: 'For God's sake, take cover; two men have just been hit within the last two seconds within a yard or two of where you are standing.'

SNOW: I see proof; their faces turned to the sky, the sand splashed with scarlet. I wait in his dugout two minutes. I must go! All the way along the lads keep calling from their dugouts: 'Get down!' 'Take cover!' 'Snipers are getting us in dozens!' I reach the captain none the worse. Snipers don't get the strength of me.

HUDDO: 'Stretcher bearers on the left', is the ceaseless cry.

TOM: April thirty.

SNOW: I cannot write—

HUDDO: It is all too terrible, too sad. Fighting still continuing with unabating fury—the men are commencing to look very weary, they do not look as if they can last much longer—

> SNOW *drops his diary pages—like the pamphlets—onto the ground.*

Little words and tiny records. Stolen moments of sanity and before the long dream of death.

SCENE EIGHTEEN

Doctor's office. SNOW *takes out a chocolate. Offers one to* TOM. TOM *accepts. They both eat the chocolates. Pause.*

SNOW: Some nights… it's a long way to go to find the dawn… We sleep under firestorm skies—wake up dead, some boys… Shipped home as pieces of paper. Never leave. Never wake. Never mind. Long way to go just to die for a bloody empire.

TOM: Are you sleeping?

SNOW: Like a corpse.

TOM: Excellent.

SNOW: Not at all.

TOM: You know why?

SNOW: Yes—I can see… I can hear… My nights are narrated by a mob of weary ghosts.

HUDDO & JOHN: [*sung*] Oh, had I the wings of a turtle dove
        I'd soar on my pinions so high
        Slap bang to the arms of my Polly love
        And in her sweet presence I'd die
ALL: [*sung*] Singing tooral liooral liaddity
        Singing tooral liooral liay
        Singing tooral liooral liaddity
        We're bound for…

SCENE NINETEEN

HUDDO: News comes to our trench.

SNOW: Our squadron leader. Shot.

JOHN: He passes on a stretcher with / some more wounded to the medical dugout.

HUDDO: At four a.m. next morning.

SNOW: We get orders to stand to arms. On the thirty-first. We relieve a battalion in Lone Pine.

TOM: How did you get up here?

SNOW: It's not easy.

TOM: I know—the trenches are narrow and the smell of the dead—

SNOW: Overwhelming…

JOHN: Warning boards written in big letters:

SNOW: 'Silence'. 'Shhh'…

> *They are under heavy artillery fire.*

> *Silence.*

> *But we see their reactions and responses to the furious noise.*

HUDDO: On the second—

JOHN: We are relieved.

SNOW: Return to headquarters.

HUDDO: We rest. On the fourth we go back to Lone Pine.

SNOW: This time with fewer men.

> SNOW *begins to roll a smoke.*

TOM: The sun is well below the horizon, the fire from the ships has died right away, the shadows deepen, until figures become moving silhouettes, or merge into the scrub which overhangs the gully. We

wait tense, expectant, like dogs on a leash—every muscle strained
for the moment of attack—

JOHN: A few whisper orders—

TOM: The loosing of the bayonet—

JOHN: I know how to shoot a gun—I know.

SNOW: We're alright, Johnny.

JOHN: What?

SNOW: We're in this together.

JOHN: Snow—

SNOW: What?

JOHN: Is this—annihilation?

HUDDO: The line will advance!

SNOW: And—then all the bloody fiends of hell let loose!

JOHN: Every rifle, every gun, opens up simultaneously!

TOM: The ridge becomes a blaze of fire! A murderous rain of lead!

SNOW: Boys wither underneath.

TOM: The wounded, screaming in agony, rolling down the sheer
slope, filling the gully below with a mass of writhing human
flesh… Soaking the gully in a torrent of blood.

HUDDO: We hang on with our bare hands to get a grip of that terrible
soil.

SNOW: It crumbles away at the touch!

HUDDO: Scrambling, rolling, sliding in our efforts to get a hold and
whilst we hang there, voiced from every throat, heard even above
their nerve wracking crash of heavy expressives rolled up the
strains of:

> TOM *and* JOHN *start singing while the dialogue continues.*

TOM & JOHN: [*sung, together*] It's a long way to Tipperary,
  It's a long way to go.
  It's a long way to Tipperary,
  To the sweetest girl I know!
  Goodbye Piccadilly,
  Farewell Leicester Square!
  It's a long long way to Tipperary,
  But my heart's right there.

> JOHN *and* TOM *continue singing through the following and all
> four continue signalling.*

SNOW: Impossible to hear orders, it's each man for himself!

HUDDO: We know what we have to do, and we do it!

SNOW: The price of peace is the bodies of our comrades and we reach the top of the ridge! In every crevice little stabs of fire, the enemy have their target in front of them, and they cannot miss!

HUDDO: They roll their bombs in dozens—at last we get them out— the ridge is taken, can we hold it?!

SNOW: A trail of lead is coming over in a solid mass, our ammunition is running out, men volunteer to supply this want, falling on the hillside as they clamber up with heavy cases, others take their place, they too fall; again come others, they fall laying among the cases, making it more difficult for those that follow to get at them!

HUDDO: Not for one second during whole of this terrible night has the enemy fire slackened.

> *The singing stops.*

At dawn the battalion is a withered remnant and the enemy—

SNOW: As always—

JOHN: Coming up in steadily increasing numbers, their supports behind them.

> *Drums.*

SNOW: The trenches are overflowing with death.

TOM: Day and night we extricate the bodies and bury them but there are still hundreds to get out. The smell is pestilential. Today we commence our seventeenth week in Gallipoli.

SNOW: So many boys lost.

TOM: The gully at the foot of the hill is filled with dead and wounded—these poor lumps of clay had once been my comrades, men I have worked and smoked and laughed and joked with—Oh God, the pity of it. It rained men in this gully; all round could be seen the sparks where the bullets were striking. Amidst this hell of writhing, mangled men and hail of bullets, a general was walking about. On my way up the hill I much wonder what I would do when I get to the top—the corporal of our signallers orders all the signallers to the rear. I go down the gully to see what I can do for some of the wounded. It is impossible to walk between them, they are in such heaps.

HUDDO: Murder, bloody murder…

TOM: One sergeant. Comes tearing along, badly wounded but full of spirits!

JOHN: 'My!'—

HUDDO: He says—

JOHN: 'But they're willing up there!'

TOM: Another poor fellow—his right hand shot away, calls out—

They stop signalling.

SNOW: 'God, but I've done my duty! I've done my duty, haven't I?'

Pause.

TOM: Yes, you have, Snow.

SCENE TWENTY

In the boat, searching with torchlights.

SNOW: Dawn. The roll is called and how heartbreaking it is—name after name is called; the reply a deep silence which is felt, despite the noise of the incessant crackling of rifles and screaming of shrapnel.

Silence.

There are few of us left to answer to our names—just a thin line of weary, ashen-faced men; behind us a mass of silent forms—they have been with me here for some days, I have not had the time to bury them. Listen!

Silence.

Nothing there—

They begin to row and see the words on the water around them.

I am tumbling all to pieces.

TOM: Simon?

SNOW *stands alone signalling with only his left hand.*

SNOW: Heliopolis. Palace Hospital. After the ceaseless thunder of guns, the agony, filth and desolation of the battlefield, it is like heaven to be tucked between clean sheets in the silence of this ward—the sisters gliding noiselessly about, the eastern architecture and decoration. I half expect to find myself wafted away on a magic carpet. Days fly into months—and here I am still in bed, and told that tonight I was discovered in one of the corridors in my delirium, imagining myself signalling.

Pause.

Somebody is leaving chocolates every other day. There is one patient who, in his delirium, is singing a series of convict songs, which is driving me mad, though to the other patients in the ward this causes considerable amusement.

Pause.

Here, as elsewhere, Death stalks—comrades pass out within a few hours of each other. One by one, they pass into the infinite. Leaving behind a name that shall ever ring glorious. As I look into the distant future when the sound of guns is but an echo I see the spirits of these my comrades in a boat with me—on water—we are searching for a noise—a sound—a voice in the darkness—friends who have handed to future generations a deeper meaning of the word—sacrifice.

SNOW *stops signalling and puts out his left hand.*

TOM *shakes hands with him this way.*

The four of them creep into the boat in silence.

SCENE TWENTY-ONE

They sit there smiling.

SNOW: And she says she's going to meet me tonight.
HUDDO: Oh, mate—I don't know how you do it.
SNOW: I'm very sincere.
TOM: You can't even spell it.
SNOW: I can.
TOM: Doesn't mean you know the meaning of the word, Snowy!
JOHN: I've got a few girls to catch up with myself.
TOM: You?
JOHN: So what?
HUDDO: You've got girlfriends?

JOHN: I've got friends who are girls.

SNOW: He was always a bit of a dark horse, I tell ya.

JOHN: I have the soul of an artist, Snowy.

SNOW: Did your mother write a note for that as well?

JOHN: Wait.

TOM: Look at those lights on the water.

SNOW: Home. This town is full of silence.

HUDDO: Nobody moving.

JOHN: Time to sleep.

TOM: Isn't it marvellous what a man can put up with—

SNOW: And yet be happy?

> *The sound of waves and distant gulls.*
>
> *They sit in silence and lights out.*

THE END

ATYP
Australian Theatre
for Young People

STATE LIBRARY
NEW SOUTH WALES

Australian Theatre for Young People and
The State Library of New South Wales
present

A Town Named War Boy

by Ross Mueller

29 April – 9 May 2015

Director
Fraser Corfield

Designer
Adrienn Lord

Lighting Designer
Emma Lockhart-Wilson

Composer
Steve Francis

Sound Designer
Alistair Wallace

Assistant Directors
Lisa Mumford and Julia Patey

Snow: **Joshua Brennan**
John: **Simon Croker**
Tom: **Brandon McClelland**
Huddo: **Edward McKenna**

FRASER CORFIELD: DIRECTOR'S NOTES

The State Library of New South Wales' collection of WWI diaries, photographs and letters is extraordinary. Having grown up with the ANZAC legend and its reference to the foundation of our nation's modern identity, I thought there was little more to be said about the landing at Gallipoli and subsequent battles. A century of books, films, poems, plays, television series and documentaries have delved into the mateship, adventure, courage, resilience and overwhelming tragedy of Australia's most famous campaign.

When you pick up one of the diaries, though, the ANZAC legend falls away. Suddenly there are just the comments, reflections and observations of a man. You can feel the indent of his pen on the page, see the corrections of thoughts, and get an insight into his personality, what makes him laugh and what inspires him. Some of the diaries take you on a personal journey through the war and returning to Australia, while others... just stop. They are an insight into young men as much they are our history. As you begin each story you have no idea at which point it will end.

Through the diaries time falls away and we are reminded of the universal qualities of young men; the sense of adventure, pride, fear, anguish, courage and loss that unites and transforms people in war. These are qualities as relevant to a 20 year old man today as they were a century ago.

The challenge in developing A Town Named War Boy has been finding a way to convey the immediacy of the experience from each diary. To that end I think playwright Ross Mueller has made some bold and very clever theatrical choices. Rather than focus on the experiences of a couple of diaries, he uses excerpts from many to provide the context for the play. These accounts become a collage narrative that takes us through the stages of the young men enlisting, travelling, and ultimately fighting at Gallipoli. This is the substance of the Gallipoli legend, the events and experiences at the heart of so many stories.

Against this backdrop Ross weaves a more abstract, contemporary story. The play becomes the journey of one man, Snow. In a recurring series of unsettling scenes, Snow repeatedly finds himself in a psychiatrist's office or adrift in a boat with his mates. While the play reflects the events of war, its heart explores the impact of war as a catalyst for change. That change is experienced by the soldiers, their families, and in the case of Gallipoli and the First World War, by all Australians. Snow struggles to remain true to the young man that sailed out of Melbourne bound for adventure, as that man has changed. Recognising and understanding this change is a torment that has plagued returned soldiers for generations.

ROSS MUELLER: WRITER'S NOTES

The brief was to write a script for a young cast on a set that can tour. Apart from that, anything was possible.

The State Library of New South Wales provided us with all possible assistance. Their staff were terrific. They know these diaries inside out. They are on a first name basis with all the authors and they talk about them like friends.

The objective was not to list battalions and military detail, but to open up the pages of the real people in the conflict. The ambition was to create characters that echo the experiences of the ANZACs, and so this play script is a stylised combination of experiences, images, words and insights from a number of voices.

As writers, these young men were poetic and economical. Their manuscripts are small; many have beautiful miniature handwriting and all of them were written under pressure. The horror of war is real. You can see this on the pages. Some days have long entries and some days are missed out completely and then some days are described with one or two words.

The stories survived Gallipoli. They brim with humour and compassion.

I feel lucky to have been able to work on this special project. I want to thank Fraser Corfield, the cast and crew of ATYP and the State Library of New South Wales for inviting me into this project.

Thanks especially to my special family – Georgie and Henry and Mum and Dad – for all your love and encouragement. It was an honour to work on this play.

ROSS MUELLER
PLAYWRIGHT

FRASER CORFIELD
DIRECTOR

Ross Mueller is a playwright, columnist, director and producer. In 2002 he was the Australian playwright at the International Residency of the Royal Court Theatre in London. In 2007, his play *The Ghost Writer* premiered at the Melbourne Theatre Company. He won the Wal Cherry Play of the Year in 2007 for *The Glory*, and in 2008 was awarded the New York New Dramatists Playwright Exchange for *Concussion*. In 2009, *Concussion* premiered at STC. In the same year, *Hard Core* was shortlisted for the Patrick White Playwrights' Award. *Construction of the Human Heart* was shortlisted for the 2007 AWGIE Award for Best New Play, nominated for five Green Room Awards, and is currently playing in Sydney presented by Apocalypse Theatre. In 2011, *ZEBRA!* premiered with a sell out season at STC. Ross reinvigorated Courthouse ARTS in Geelong as Artistic Director, turning it into a vibrant arts community. He has also worked on commissions and developments with St Martin's, Canberra Youth Theatre and Back to Back Theatre. He has worked extensively with ATYP's Fresh Ink program and as a tutor at the National Studio. He is undertaking his master's degree at the Victorian College of the Arts.

Fraser Corfield is the Artistic Director of ATYP. He has been the Artistic Director of Backbone Youth Arts (Qld, 2005-2008) and Riverland Youth Theatre (SA, 2001-2003), and the Associate Director of La Boite Theatre (1997-2000). He has staged work in partnership with many of the country's flagship companies and festivals. As an Artistic Director, Fraser has commissioned and produced over thirty new plays and productions. Highlights include *M.Rock* (ATYP/STC), *Sugarland* (ATYP), *The Tender Age* (ATYP/version 1.0), Australia's first major opera for young people *Dirty Apple* (Backbone Youth Arts/Opera Queensland/Queensland Music Festival), the new Australian musical *Paradise* (Backbone Youth Arts), and AWGIE award-winning plays *Grounded* by Alana Valentine (2013 ATYP/Tantrum Theatre) and *I Said a Word* by Stephen House (2002 Riverland Youth Theatre). Over the past twenty years, Fraser has directed productions for professional, independent and youth theatre companies around Australia. For ATYP he has directed *Sugarland, M.Rock, Spur of the Moment, Max Remy Super Spy, Ishmael and the Return of the Dugongs, The Tender Age* (co-directed with David Williams), *Desiree Dinn and the Red Forest, Rio Saki and Other Falling Debris*, and *The Laramie Project*.

ADRIENN LORD
DESIGNER

Adrienn Lord is a set and costume designer for theatre, events, film and television. Adrienn has always had a passion for bringing people together through communal experiences. He consistently strives for new, elegant and potent forms of expression in space, and with colours and materials, to support and further articulate inspiring narrative and concept.

Adrienn has designed and assisted for The Really Useful Group, Sydney Theatre Company, Global Creatures, Australian Theatre for Young People, Darlinghurst Theatre, Q Theatre, Tamarama Rock Surfers, Arts Radar, Harbour City Opera and Owl Farm. His commercial works have included clients such as Westfield Shopping Centres, Macquarie Shopping Centre, and the Newtown Hotel.

Adrienn is a graduate of NIDA's Design Course, including a collaborative film with AFTRS, and Events and Entertainment Design from the Design Centre, Enmore. He graduated with the highest mark statewide, and was nominated for an Outstanding Achievement Award in competition with all TAFE NSW courses.

EMMA LOCKHART-WILSON
LIGHTING DESIGNER

Emma Lockhart-Wilson is a production graduate of the University of Wolllongong Bachelor of Creative Arts and holds a Master in Design from the College of Fine Arts (UNSW). Emma is also resident designer with emerging performance collective His Three Daughters, who have shown work at Woodcourt Art Theatre, Adelaide Fringe Festival, Crack Theatre Festival (TINA) and You Are Here Arts Festival.

Lighting Designs include *Make a Band* (Applespiel/ Malthouse Helium Program), *Out of Line* and *Late Night Shopping* (Shopfront), *Ragnarök/or how it ended/* and *Carly and Troy Do 'A Doll's House'* (His Three Daughters), *Framed* (De Quincey Co.), *Debris* (Bodysnatchers), *Platform 3* and *Platform 4* (The Weather Exchange), *Harvest*, *Beguiled* and *Unsettlings* (PACT), *Of the Causes of Wonderful Things* (Talya Rubin) and *Seven Kilometres North-East* (version 1.0).

STEVE FRANCIS
COMPOSER

Steve Francis is a composer for the theatre, screen and dance. As a composer for theatre, Steve has created work for Sydney Theatre Company, Belvoir Theatre, Bell Shakespeare, Griffin Theatre, ATYP, the Melbourne Theatre Company and the State Theatre Company of South Australia. For dance, Steve has composed five full length works for Bangarra Dance, including the award-winning *Walkabout*. He has also composed for the Australian Ballet. Steve has composed for a number of films, including *The Turning*, the multi-award-winning *dik*, Leah Purcell's *She Say*, the Dendy Award-winning film *Black Talk*, Berlin Festival-winner *Djarn Djarns* and the Melbourne Film Festival Award-winning documentary *Mr Patterns*. Steve also produced and composed music for *Awakenings*, the Indigenous section of the Sydney Olympic Games Opening Ceremony, as well as *Earth* for the Rugby World Cup Opening. His awards include Helpmann Awards for Best Original Score in 2012 and 2003, as well as Best New Australian Work in 2003. He has also won two Sydney Theatre Awards for Music and Sound Design in 2014 and 2011, and was nominated for a Screen Composers Guild award, 2008.

ALISTAIR WALLACE
SOUND DESIGNER

Alistair Wallace is an actor, producer, comedian and sound designer. He graduated from the Actors Centre Australia in 2010 and is a founding member and artistic associate of pantsguys Productions. Alistair's sound design credits include: *Platonov* (MopHead and Catnip Productions); *Jerusalem* (New Theatre, nominated Best Independent Sound Design, Sydney Theatre Awards 2013), *Punk Rock* (pantsguys Productions, presented by ATYP Under the Wharf, winner of Best Independent Production, Sydney Theatre Awards 2012), *Through These Lines* (TAP productions), *The Memory of Us* (Ashfield Council), *When the Rain Stops Falling*, *Harvest*, *Small Poppies*, *Lord of the Flies* (New Theatre), *Mr Kolpert*, *The Shape of Things* (pantsguys Productions, presented by ATYP Under the Wharf) and *autobahn* (pantsguys/Adelaide Fringe).

LISA MUMFORD
ASSISTANT DIRECTOR

JULIA PATEY
ASSISTANT DIRECTOR

Lisa Mumford is ATYP's Education Co-ordinator. She has worked as a performer and co-devisor within the collective Friends with Deficits. Within this collective she has performed for Brisbane Festival's Under the Radar in *In Light of a Moon*, and with the same show as part of Sydney's Art and About festival. Friends with Deficits has also performed another species entirely for Tamarama Rock Surfers at the Old Fitzroy, as part of Freshly Squeezed and Fruit at The Paper Mill. Friends with Deficits created *On Romance*, which was developed through the PACT theatre residency program Vacant Room, and has been shown in various incarnations as part of Beams Festival Chippendale, The Rocks Village Night Bizarre and Crack Theatre Festival. The trio has curated for Performance Space's NightTime, and are currently developing a new work for Underbelly Arts festival 2015. Lisa holds a degree in Performance Studies and Education and has trained with the Ensemble at PACT theatre. She also works as an occasional florist.

Julia Patey is an emerging director, playwright and theatre-maker. Julia's work has been performed in theatres, pubs and backyards across Australia, including: The Blue Room Theatre, Holden Street Theatre and ATYP. Julia's work with ATYP includes: Assistant Director, *Spur of the Moment* (2013), and Young Playwright, National Studio (2014). In 2015, Julia was commissioned to write 'Sure', for The Voices Project: *Between Us*, published by Currency Press.

As an independent theatre-maker, producer and director, Julia's work includes new works: *We Are All, The Hand of Time* (Not Suitable for Drinking), *Where There's Smoke/Burnt* (99seats Theatre), and *Stockholm*. As Assistant Director: *The Magic Hour* (Performing Lines WA).

Julia is a graduate of Charles Sturt University, Bathurst (Theatre/Media) and is a proud recipient of The Blair Milan Memorial Scholarship, which she was awarded in 2013 for her production *Burnt*. Julia is a founding member of 99seats Theatre, and resident director for Not Suitable for Drinking, a theatre collective dedicated to producing new writing with emerging artists.

Julia is currently undertaking a playwriting mentorship with ATYP as a part of Fresh Ink and is thrilled to be part of *A Town Named War Boy*.

JOSHUA BRENNAN
ACTOR

SIMON CROKER
ACTOR

Joshua Brennan graduated from the Western Australian Academy of Performing Arts (WAAPA) in 2011. Television credits include *Ocean Star*, *Castaway*, ABC telemovie *The Shark Net* alongside William McInnes, and *Underbelly: Badness* (Nine Network). On stage, *M.Rock* (STC/ATYP), *Spur of the Moment* (ATYP), *Tender Napalm* (Perth Theatre Company), Heath Ledger Theatre Gala Opening for the WA State Theatre Company and *Up in the Flood* (Black Swan Theatre Company). In 2013, Joshua was seen in *Home and Away* on the Seven Network, and the ABC telemovie, *Parer's War*.

Simon Croker graduated from the Australian Film, Television and Radio School in 2014. His theatre credits include *Dead Man Walking* (State Theatre) and in the role of Hans in *Werther* (Opera Australia). While studying at AFTRS last year he also devised and performed in *God Save the Queen* at the Melbourne Fringe Festival. *A Town Named War Boy* marks his first production with ATYP.

BRANDON McCLELLAND
ACTOR

Brandon McClelland is an Australian actor who has appeared on stage, in television and film. Brandon graduated from NIDA in 2012. In 2014, he appeared in ATYP/Sydney Theatre Company's *M.Rock*, and in 2015, STC's *Suddenly Last Summer*. On television, he is best known for his portrayal of Pat Dooley on ABC TV's *ANZAC Girls*, Nine Network's *Love Child*, and Foxtel's *Devil's Playground*. He recently completed filming on the US feature film *Truth*.

EDWARD McKENNA
ACTOR

Edward McKenna, proud to have grown up in Sydney's western suburbs, began his training at the Sydney Theatre School. He was lucky enough to have worked with such directors as Cristabell Sved, Michael Piggot and Malcolm Frawley, before continuing his training at The Actors Centre Australia, from which he graduated in 2014. Some highlights during his training include: Ivanov in Anton Chekov's *Ivanov*, directed by Joseph Uchitel; Lysander in William Shakespeare's *A Midsummer Night's Dream*, directed by Jennifer West and George Ogilvie; Danny in John Patrick Shanley's *Danny and the Deep Blue Sea*; and Ogun in T*he Brothers Size*, directed by Adam Cook. Other theatre appearances include Kirill in Anton Chekov's *Platonov*, directed by Anthony Skuse and more recently, Arman in Christopher Bryant's *Sixty-Three Days*, directed by David Burrowes. *Sixty-Three Days* formed apart of Apocalypse Theatre Company's quick response show, *Asylum*. Edward also enjoys writing and directing his own short films. He is absolutely thrilled to be working with ATYP and thankful for being given the chance to work on a new Australian text.

ABOUT AUSTRALIAN THEATRE FOR YOUNG PEOPLE

A Town Named War Boy has been commissioned and developed by the Australian Theatre for Young People (ATYP) in partnership with the State Library of New South Wales.

As Australia's national youth theatre company, ATYP is one of the world's oldest and largest theatre companies dedicated to putting young people centre stage.

At the heart of ATYP's process is the collaboration between industry leaders and young artists. Whether it is the development of a major production or the facilitation of a community workshop, it is the interests, ideas and passion of young people that is our reason for being.

Alongside our main stage work, ATYP takes a leadership role in showcasing work with young people on national stages. Over the past three years, we have partnered with most of Australia's flagship companies and venues. Our programmes have been delivered in partnership with companies in every state and territory in Australia and our online resources have been seen by over 1 million people around the world.

ATYP is thrilled to work with the State Library of New South Wales and we are delighted to have *A Town Named War Boy* as part of our 2015 season.

We hope you enjoy this funny, moving and intimate play by Ross Mueller.

ATYP
Australian Theatre
for Young People

Supported by the ATYP Producers' Circle

NSW GOVERNMENT | Trade & Investment Arts NSW

Australian Government

Australia Council for the Arts

STATE LIBRARY OF NEW SOUTH WALES

The State Library of NSW is one of the great libraries of the world, with a history dating back to 1826. Its renowned historical and contemporary collections, comprising more than five million items – books, manuscripts, maps, photographs, paintings, architectural plans and online content – hold the growing memory of our state and nation.

The Library's first collection of 236 soldiers' diaries was acquired as part of an extraordinary collecting drive from 1918 to 1920. It was recently included on the UNESCO Australian Memory of the World Register, joining the Holtermann Collection and First Fleet journals. The Library's First World War collection has grown to include over 1,200 handwritten diaries and letters by soldiers, doctors, nurses, stretcher-bearers, journalists and POWs.

The story of the First World War cannot be fully understood without reference to these personal and moving records. Such is their cultural significance, these diaries have become a source of inspiration for many artistic and literary works and educational programs around Australia commemorating the centenary of the First World War.

This collaboration with the Australian Theatre for Young People showcases the diaries in an exciting new way. Ross Mueller's new Australian play, *A Town Named War Boy*, interprets the compelling stories held within these first-hand accounts for a contemporary audience.

Throughout the centenary, the Library will continue to share the day-to-day experiences of the Australian men and women who served, through onsite and online exhibitions, public events and regional outreach and education programs.

P

STATE LIBRARY
NEW SOUTH WALES

www.ingramcontent.com/pod-product-compliance
Lightning Source LLC
Chambersburg PA
CBHW050024090426

42734CB00021B/3410